What's So Funny?

Silly Stickers, Wacky Jokes, Funny Posters, Crazy Photos, and More!

by Trula Magruder and Chris Lorette David
Illustrated by Lauren Scheuer

★ American Girl®

Published by American Girl Publishing, Inc.

Copyright © 2008 by American Girl, LLC

Questions or comments? Call 1-800-845-0005,
visit our Web site at **americangirl.com**,
or write to Customer Service, American Girl,
8400 Fairway Place, Middleton, WI 53562-0497.

Printed in China

11 12 13 14 15 16 LEO 13 12 11 10 9 8 7

Editorial Development: Trula Magruder and Chris Lorette David;
Art Direction: Chris Lorette David;
Production: Jeannette Bailey, Judith Lary, Sarah Boecher,
Gretchen Krause, Mindy Rappe, Tami Kepler

Illustrations: Lauren Scheuer

Dear Reader,

We all love to laugh, and nothing feels better than *sharing* a laugh. Inside this book you'll find lots of funny pages to tear and share with friends and family.

• Read the strange stories to your family in the car.
• Pass around the funny photos at a slumber party.
• Recite the riddles at recess.
• Draw the daffy designs with a friend on the bus.
• Discover nutty names with a sibling.

So share a smile! You'll make the world just a little brighter.

Your friends at American Girl

Rock On!

Column 1

A = Angry

B = Bearded

C = CRAZY

D = Die-hard

E = Electric

F = Flaming

G = Grim

H = Heavy

I = Indigo

J = Jealous

K = K-9

L = Liquid

M = MOODY

N = Ninety-Nine

O = Organic

P = Plastic

Q = QUAKING

R = Rhythmic

S = Screaming

T = Three-D

U = Undercover

V = Velvet

W = Wooden

X = X-Ray

Y = Young

Z = Zodiac

You might not have a hard-rock band, but you can have a band name. Try this for laughs: Find your first initial in column 1 and your last initial in column 2. Hey, cool band!

Column 2

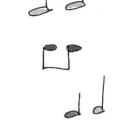

A = Angels

B = Bettys

C = Cupid

D = Dogs

E = Elephants

F = FISH

G = Girls

H = Heart

I = Ice

J = Jungle

K = Kids

L = Lizards

M = MONKEYS

N = Nurses

O = Orange

P = PUPPETS

Q = Queen

R = Rain

S = Strawberries

T = Toast

U = UFOs

V = Veronicas

W = Wreckers

X = Xmas

Y = Yearbooks

Z = Zombies

If Animals Could Talk

Choose a caption from the list below to fill in the speech bubble at right—or make up your own caption! Hang the poster in a school locker or in your room.

- I'd like a large cheese pizza . . . hold the pizza.
- Oh, look! The Cheese House is on speed dial!
- Can you hear me now?

Fowl Funnies

These riddles will get you clucking!

What bird is always out of breath? A puffin • What bird carries the most weight? A crane • What bird is at every meal? A swallow • What bird is the best ball-player? A flycatcher • Why does the flamingo stand with one leg off the ground? Because if she lifted both legs, she'd be sitting • Why do pelicans carry fresh fish in their beaks? Because they don't have pockets • On which day do birds celebrate their dads? Feather's Day • Where do birds go on vacation? To the Canary Islands • What is smarter than a talking parrot? A spelling bee • Why did the egg get thrown out of school? It kept telling yolks.

Great "yolks"!

Look on page 83 for Fowl Funny stickers to decorate your school supplies or to share with your friends.

Tricky Doodles

Figure out the word or words in these odd art pieces.

1. _____

2. _____

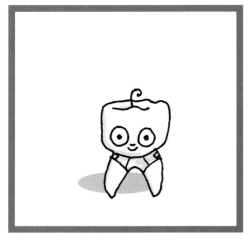

3. _____

4. _____

Oh, yeah. The answers are in this book somewhere.

Daffy Designer

Design a surfboard to give this princess a royal ride.

Wig Out!

Remove the blank face at right, slip your photo behind the wig, tape the photo in place, and then proudly display!

Strange News Stories 1

Part 1: Fill in the blanks, and then turn to page 17.

1. Name your **city and state.**

2. Make up a **nonsense word.**

3. Jot down a **small number.**

4. Write in the name of a **shape.**

5. Choose a **noun.**

6. Write down your favorite **TV ad slogan.**

7. Fill in an **-ing action verb.**

8. What's your favorite **color?**

9. What's your favorite **food?**

10. Choose another **-ing action verb.**

11. Pencil in a **noise.**

12. Come up with a **plural noun.**

Guess What!

What is this?
(Look below to read our analysis.)

A zebra in an earthquake

Meet
What's-Her-Face

Look on page 85 for reusable stickers to complete this girl's look.

Strange News Stories 1

NASA reported today that an alien species has landed

on Earth near _____.

1

Scientists have decided to call the aliens

_____. Typical aliens appear

2

to have _____ arm(s) and _____ legs, and

3   4

they wear a _____ on their heads. So far, the

5

aliens have repeated one phrase, although no one is sure how they heard it:

" _____

6

_____."

The aliens move from one place to the other by _____.

7

They like to eat a food that looks like _____ _____.

8   9

The noise they make when they're _____

10

sounds like " _____." At this stage, scientists

11

are asking people to avoid alien contact because the aliens have been known

to turn things into _____.

12

If Animals Could Talk

Choose a caption from the list below to fill in the speech bubble at right—or make up your own caption! Hang the poster in a school locker or in your room.

- This sprinkled doughnut tastes kinda funny.
- Last one into the pool's a rotten egg!
- It's a little uncomfortable, but apparently this is what all the poodles in Paris are wearing.

A Season of Smiles

Jokes to read all year long

What do you call a person who sells flowers? A petal pusher • Why do flowers seem so lazy? They're usually in a bed. • **Why do spiders spin webs? Because they can't knit them** • What insects are difficult to understand? Mumble bees • **What do you call a snowman in the summer? Puddle** • How do squirrels know it's fall? Because the trees leaf the forest • **What do turkeys say after they walk in circles? Wobble, wobble** • What cars did the pilgrims drive? *Autumn*obiles • Why did the snowman fall in love with the sunbeam? She melted his heart. • **Why are snowmen always round? Because if they were square, they'd be ice cubes** • What's white and black . . . and white and black . . . and white and black? A penguin rolling down an iceberg • **Where do ducks sleep when it rains? On water beds** • What do businessmen often wear when it's raining? Wet suits

Now, that's funny!

Tear out the poster at right and hang it where you can see it when you need a quick chuckle.

Wig Out!

Remove the blank face at right, slip your photo behind the wig, tape the photo in place, and then proudly display!

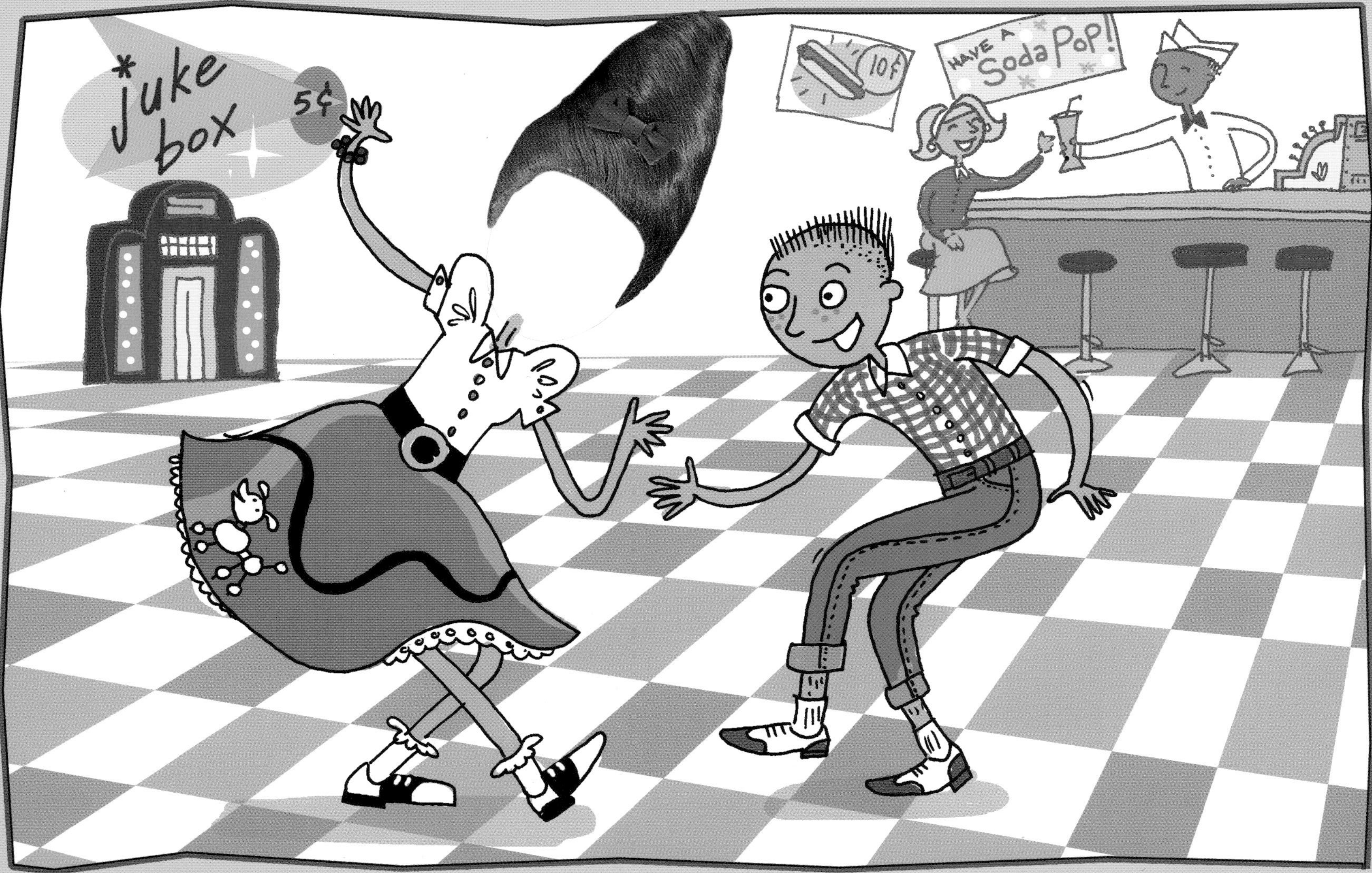

*Juke box
5¢
10¢
HAVE A Soda Pop!

Daffy Designer

Design a dream cage for Petunia (the dwarf hamster).

Animal Accessories 1

You'll find stickers on page 87 [...] plete the penguin's look.

Tricky Doodles

Figure out the word or words in these odd art pieces.

1. _____

2. _____

3. _____

Your turn!

4. ___ *sunfish* ___

Need the answers? They're not on this page!

Act Like . . .

Giddyup!

Column 1

A = Austin

B = Billie

C = CODY

D = Dixie

E = Ellie

F = Fanny

G = Gabby

H = Hart

I = Ida

J = Jess

K = KENDALL

L = Logan

M = MISSY

N = Nell

O = Orlene

P = Preston

Q = QUINN

R = Red

S = Slim

T = Trey

U = Uriah

V = Virginia

W = Wyoming

X = Xander

Y = Yvonne

Z = Zora

Act like . . .

1. a duck on caffeine.
2. a superhero who fights crime on her tiptoes.
3. a news reporter who talks v-e-r-y slowly.
4. a fashion model on a slippery runway.
5. a shy police officer who likes to give tickets.
6. a teacher who sings her lessons.
7. a monkey who believes that people are in a zoo.
8. an alien who tries to communicate with stuffed animals, thinking that they inhabit Earth.

9   a weather reporter who must fill two minutes on the air about a sunny day.

10   a girl who treats a sock puppet as her pet.

11   a baby taking her first steps.

12   a bored cheerleader at a losing game.

13   a detective who freezes in a funny pose as soon as someone comes near.

14   a person who must sell a product that she secretly hates and doesn't want anyone to buy.

15   a clumsy waitress.

Has anyone ever told you that you act silly? Well, here's your big chance to do it again. To receive your role, follow the instructions written below.

Pick a number from 1 to 15, write it below, and then open up this page to see what you need to do.

_____

If you plan to head west, visit a dude ranch, or ride a horse, you'll need a cowgirl name. To find yours, use your first initial in column 1 and your last initial in column 2. What's your name, partner?

Column 2

A = Autry

B = Blair

C = Carson

D = Dixon

E = Evans

F = FLOYD

G = Garrett

H = Hickok

I = Indiana

J = James

K = Kid

L = Lane

M = MCCOY

N = Nash

O = Oakley

P = PICKENS

Q = Quaid

R = Rider

S = Shiloh

T = Tucker

U = Utah

V = Valley

W = Walker

X = Xavier

Y = Young

Z = Zane

If Animals Could Talk

Choose a caption from the list below to fill in the speech bubble at right—or make up your own caption! Hang the poster in a school locker or in your room.

- I just hate growing out my bangs.
- Ponytails? Pigtails? No wonder I'm having a bad hair day—no one's invented bulltails!
- Hello, is this Bull's Beauty Shop? I need an appointment. Yes, it's an emergency!

Chicken Chuckles

Why did the girl cross the road? To read these riddles!

Why did the chicken cross the road, roll in dirt, turn around, and come back? She was a dirty double-crosser. • Why did the rubber chicken cross the road? She wanted to stretch her legs. • How did the rich rubber chicken cross the road? In her stretch limo • Why did the fish cross the road? To get to her school • Why did the rabbits cross the road? To get to the hopping center • Why did the turkey cross the road? To prove she wasn't chicken • Why did the otter cross the road? To get to the otter side • Why did the wolf cross the road? He wanted chicken for dinner. • Why did the letter A cross the road? Because a B was right behind her! • Why did the dinosaur cross the road? Because chickens weren't invented yet • Why did the snail cross the road? We're still waiting . . . We'll let you know once it has arrived. • Why did the computer cross the road? Because the chicken programmed it to cross • Why did the scientific chicken cross the road? To invent the other side

Are you laughing at Me?

Tear out the poster at right and hang it where you can see it when you need a quick chuckle.

Why did the chicken stop crossing the road?

She got tired of all the chicken jokes!

Wig Out!

Remove the blank face at right, slip your photo behind the wig, tape the photo in place, and then proudly display!

Tongue Twisters

Butterflies flutter by famously.

Six sick sheep

A cup of proper coffee in a copper coffee cup

Aluminum linoleum

Dreary, Dear, Dreary

Toy boat

A big black bug bit a big black bear.

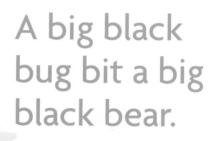

Unique New York

unique!

Please free foreign fleas.

A skunk sat on a stump. The stump thunk the skunk stunk and the skunk thunk the stump stunk.

Mighty mites blindly bite mightily.

Happily, the classy grasshopper happened to hip-hop.

Six slick slugs shivered silently.

Rubber baby buggy bumpers

Tricky Doodles

1. _____

2. _____

3. _____

Your turn!

4. _____ *firefly* _____

Figure out the word or words in these odd art pieces.

5. _____

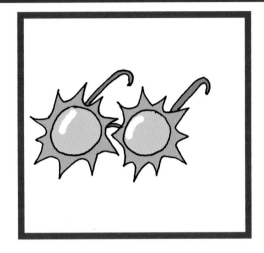

6. _____

7. _____

Your turn!

8. __ladybug__

Here's even more work: Find the answers!

Daffy Designer

Design a hot-air balloon that will give this cowgirl a wild ride!

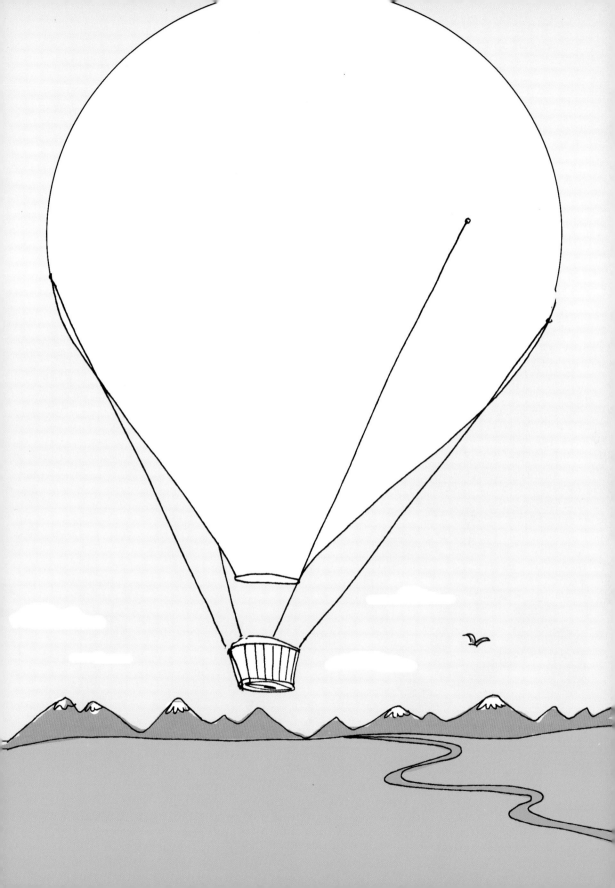

Wig Out!

Remove the blank face at right, slip your photo behind the wig, tape the photo in place, and then proudly display!

Choose a caption from the list below to fill in the speech bubble at right—or make up your own caption! Hang the poster in a school locker or in your room.

- C'mon. Just one little kiss?

- Eww! That must have hurt! You gotta watch out for those banana peels.

- I'm gonna teach all apes how to whistle.

Let's Goo!

Column 1

A = Applesauce

B = Bubblegum

C = CHOCOLATE

D = Doughnut

E = Egg

F = Foam

G = Gravy

H = Honey

I = Ice Cream

J = Jell-O

K = KETCHUP

L = Licorice

M = MUD

N = Nougat

O = Oil

P = Pudding

Q = QUICKSAND

R = Raisin

S = Sticky

T = Toothpaste

U = Unfrozen Popsicle

V = Vaseline

W = Whipped Cream

X = MAKE UP YOUR OWN!

Y = Yogurt

Z = Ziti pasta

Surprise the world with a slimy, silly family fun house! To name your gooey adventure, use your first initial in column 1 and your last initial in column 2. Will your event draw a crowd?

Column 2

A = Arcade

B = Beach

C = Camp

D = Dells

E = Eatery

F = FARM

G = Gardens

H = Hotel

I = Igloo

J = Jungle

K = Kingdom

L = Library

M = MALL

N = Nation

O = Observatory

P = PARK

Q = Quarter

R = Ranch

S = Shores

T = Theater

U = University

V = Village

W = Water Park

X = MAKE UP YOUR OWN!

Y = Yards

Z = Zoo

Strange News Stories 2

Part 1: Fill in the blanks, and then turn to pages 74–75.

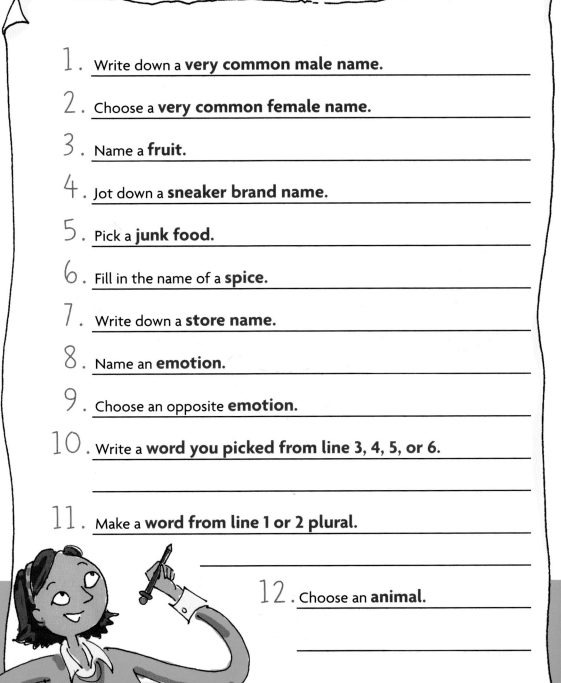

1. Write down a **very common male name.** _____

2. Choose a **very common female name.** _____

3. Name a **fruit.** _____

4. Jot down a **sneaker brand name.** _____

5. Pick a **junk food.** _____

6. Fill in the name of a **spice.** _____

7. Write down a **store name.** _____

8. Name an **emotion.** _____

9. Choose an opposite **emotion.** _____

10. Write a **word you picked from line 3, 4, 5, or 6.** _____
_____

11. Make a **word from line 1 or 2 plural.** _____
_____

12. Choose an **animal.** _____
_____

Animal Accessories 2

SHERIFF

What is this?
(See what we thought below.)

A girl riding her bike really fast down a very bumpy road

Daffy Designer

Design a tour bus for this beautiful ballerina!

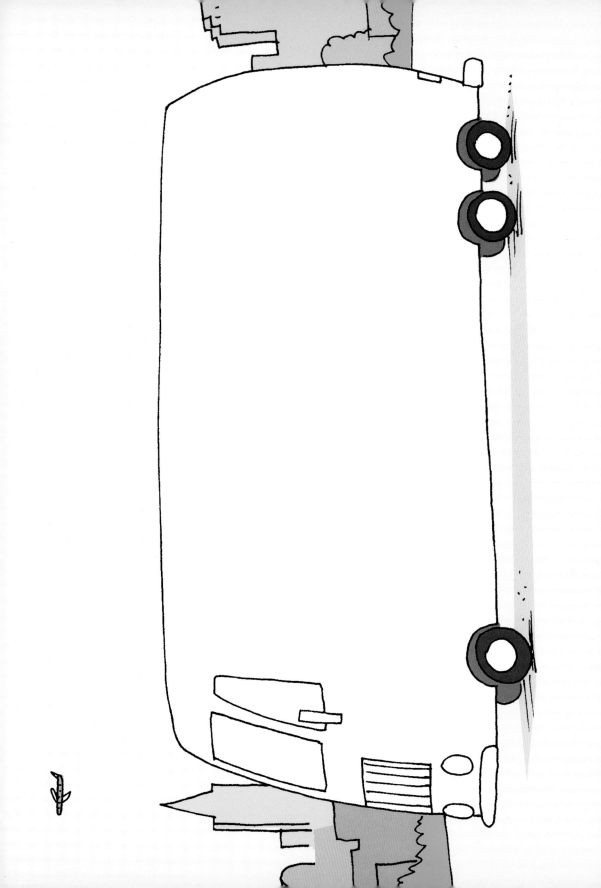

If Animals Could Talk

Choose a caption from the list below to fill in the speech bubble at right—or make up your own caption! Hang the poster in a school locker or in your room.

- I know plastic surgery is popular, but honestly, I think you've gone too far.

- Listen, if you want to get anywhere, you must paddle your feet.

- I understand that you're shy, but could you please say something?

Why is it a good idea to plant bulbs in your garden? So worms can see where they're going • What do you call a mean insect? A bitter-fly • What did one flea say to the other flea? Should we walk or do you want to take the dog? • Why did Noah's ark sink? Because he brought along two termites • What did the depressed caterpillar decide to do on New Year's Day? Turn over a new leaf • Why do bees have sticky hair? Because they use honeycombs • What's a butterfly's favorite subject? *Moth*ematics • What kind of barbecue grill does a spider like? A *Weber*! • What did the spider couple say to the fly? When we get married, do you want to come to the webbing? • What insect lives in a gum tree? A stick bug! • Where do bees go on vacation? The wax museum

That would be a knee-slapper . . . if I had a knee.

For more bug laughs, look for the stickers on page 93.

Tricky Doodles

Figure out the word or words in these odd art pieces.

1. _____

2. _____

3. _____

Your turn!

4. __ **boxcar** ____

Oh, yeah. The answers are in this book . . . somewhere.

59

Wig Out!

Remove the blank face at right, slip your photo behind the wig, tape the photo in place, and then proudly display!

QUEEN of the NILE

Wild Life!

Column 1

A = Autumn

B = Brave

C = CHARGING

D = Daughter

E = Earth

F = Fire

G = Great

H = Healing

I = Iron

J = Jumping

K = KIND

L = Lone

M = MOON

N = Night

O = One

P = **Peace**

Q = QUIET

R = Rainbow

S = Spirit

T = Thunder

U = Upstream

V = Village

W = Winter

X = FREE SPACE! YOU CHOOSE!

Y = Young

Z = Zigzagging

Wild about the environment? Now you can pick a wilderness name to promote your passion. To find it, use your first initial in column 1 and your last initial in column 2. Ready to roam the earth?

Column 2

A = Alligator

B = Bear

C = Coyote

D = Deer

E = Eagle

F = FOX

G = Gazelle

H = Horse

I = Iguana

J = Jaguar

K = Koala

L = Lion

M = MONGOOSE

N = Nighthawk

O = Otter

P = PANTHER

Q = Quail

R = Rabbit

S = Salmon

T = Tortoise

U = Unicorn

V = Vulture

W = Wolf

X = FREE SPACE! YOU CHOOSE!

Y = Yellow Jacket

Z = Zebra

Fortune Teller

Pick two numbers from 1 to 25.
Write them below and then open
up this page to see your fortune.

A_____

B_____

Tricky Doodles

1. _____

2. _____

3. _____

Your turn!

4. **redhead**

Something unique will happen to you soon. To gaze into the future and see what and with whom, follow the instructions below. Surprised?

You will . . .

A

1. explore with
2. yo-yo with
3. make friends with
4. dine with
5. quarrel with
6. shop with
7. garden with
8. play with
9. interview
10. vacation with
11. zone out with
12. learn from
13. craft with
14. offer help to
15. negotiate with
16. hiccup in front of
17. assist
18. read to
19. fly with
20. teach
21. unwrap gifts from
22. journey with
23. write to
24. babysit for
25. kid around with

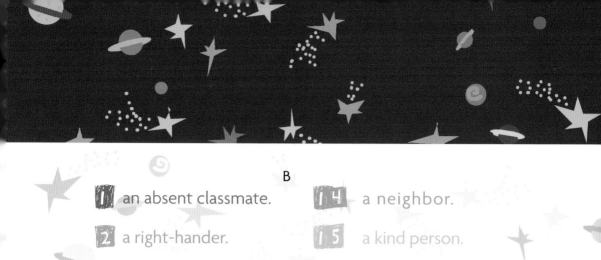

B

1 an absent classmate.

2 a right-hander.

3 a teacher.

4 a dreamer.

5 a visitor.

6 a family friend.

7 a young animal.

8 an honor student.

9 an identical twin.

10 a zany store clerk.

11 an older person.

12 a left-hander.

13 a musician.

14 a neighbor.

15 a kind person.

16 a poet.

17 a quiet friend.

18 a best friend.

19 a sibling.

20 a contest winner.

21 an uncle or aunt.

22 an eleven-year-old.

23 a writer.

24 a girlfriend.

25 an athlete.

Figure out the word or words in these odd art pieces.

5. _____

6. _____

7. _____

Your turn!

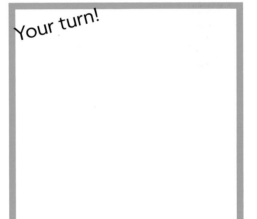

8. ___*sunflower*___

Getting closer, but the answers are farther ahead.

Guess What!

What is this?
(See our answer below. Agree?)

Penguins on a really hot day!

And this?
(We could be wrong, but check out our answer below.)

A goldfish's view of a cat looking into her aquarium

School Snickers

Finally, some jokes with class.

What did the math book say to the psychiatrist? I've got a lot of problems! • What did the ghostly teacher say to her class? Look at the board and I'll go through it again. • Why did the student bring her father to school? Because the teacher told her they would be having a *pop* quiz • Where do female monsters study? At a ghouls' school • What do you get when you cross a vampire with a teacher? Lots of blood tests • If witches went to school, what would be their best subject? *Spell*ing • What did the clock in the cafeteria do when it was still hungry? It went back for seconds! • What kinds of pets do librarians prefer? Book-worms • Why did the school cancel the baseball game? Because everyone ran home • What do skeletons like to earn for school? *Skull*erships! • Where does a yodeler go to get an education? *Yell*-ementary school

Get it? Yell-ementary school!

Tear out the poster at right and hang it where you can see it when you need a quick chuckle.

What's the most powerful
school supply?

The ruler

Meet
Whats-Its-Face

Look on page 95 for stickers to complete this monsterous look.

Tricky Doodles Answers

You found them!

page 9: 1. shoe store   2. feather bed   3. baby tooth   4. teacup

page 27: 1. keyboard   2. bookstore   3. football

pages 40–41: 1. footstool   2. catfish   3. handbag

 5. sandbox   6. sunglasses   7. rock band

page 59: 1. cupcake   2. baseball mitt   3. pumpkin patch

pages 66–67: 1. bottle cap   2. pigpen   3. horsefly

 5. ballroom   6. raincoats   7. copycats

Strange News Stories 2

The parents of four children, who themselves are

named Mr. _____ Smith and

Mrs. _____ Smith, decided to

spice up their lives by naming their children after

common household items. The couple chose to name

their oldest daughter _____,

her brother _____,

another daughter _____,

and a little brother _____.

The family says that the names attract a lot of atten-

tion, especially at _____.

"I feel _____ about it, but I think

my sister feels _____ about

9

it," says _____. "Still,

10

we're a unique family, so it's nice to have unique

names. After all, the world isn't just filled with

_____!" The parents

11

say they don't regret their name choices at all.

"In fact, if we have another child,

we think we'll call him or her

"_____,"

12

says Mr. Smith.

Crazy Café

Column 1

A = Adventurous

B = Bruised

C = CHARMING

D = Delicate

E = Enchanted

F = Fancy

G = **Green**

H = Hungry

I = Itchy

J = Jubilant

K = KOOKY

L = Lazy

M = MYSTERIOUS

N = Natural

O = Olympic

P = **Purple**

Q = QUIRKY

R = Restless

S = Sticky

T = Thai

U = Urban

V = Vital

W = Worthy

X = DINER'S CHOICE!

Y = Young

Z = Zesty

76

If you plan to open a vegetarian diner one day, you'll need a crazy name to draw curious customers. To find one, use your first initial in column 1 and your last initial in column 2. What's your café called?

Column 2

A = Avocado

B = Beet

C = Carrot

D = Dip

E = Eggplant

F = FIGS

G = Grains

H = Honeydew

I = Iceberg

J = Jalapeno

K = Kiwi

L = Lemon

M = MACARONI

N = Noodles

O = Olive

P = PEPPER

Q = Quiche

R = Radish

S = Spinach

T = Tofu

U = Ugli™ Fruit

V = Vegan

W = Watermelon

X = DINER'S CHOICE!

Y = Yam

Z = Zucchini

If Animals Could Talk

Choose a caption from the list below to fill in the speech bubble at right—or make up your own caption! Hang the poster in a school locker or in your room.

- Oh, man! That last cold salmon gave me a brain freeze!
- The paparazzi can be so annoying.
- Aw, shucks. Now you're embarrassing me.

We see that
you want to write to us.
Send your letters to:

What's So Funny? Editor
American Girl
8400 Fairway Place
Middleton, WI 53562

(All comments and suggestions received
by American Girl may be used without
compensation or acknowledgment.
Sorry—photos can't be returned.)

Guess What!

What is this?
(Look below. We try to be funny.)

The dog-gone end!

Here are some other American Girl books you might like:

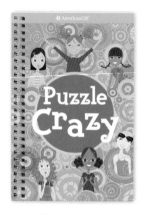

❑ I read it.

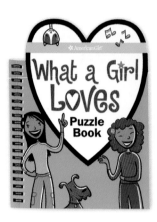

❑ I read it.

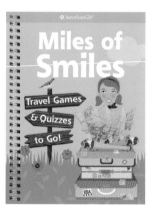

❑ I read it.

❑ I read it.

❑ I read it.

❑ I read it.